AI TRENDS

By 2030, artificial intelligence and machine learning are expected to replace 16% of all US jobs.

— FORRESTER

97 million people will work in AI-related industries by 2025.

— EXPLODING TOPICS

In 2023, weekly job posts related to generative AI increased by nearly 450% compared to 2022.

— UPWORK

Two months after its launch (November 2022), ChatGPT had reached a whopping 100 million monthly active users.

— SIMILARWEB

101 AI JOB IDEAS

FROM CAREERS TO SIDE HUSTLES

NICE MACHINE AI PUBLISHING

NICE MACHINE AI PUBLISHING

Copyright © 2023 by Nice Machine AI Publishing

All rights reserved.

No part of this book may be reproduced in any form or by any electronic or mechanical means, including information storage and retrieval systems, without written permission from the author, except for the use of brief quotations in a book review.

Disclosure

WE MAY RECEIVE AN AFFILIATE COMMISSION—at no additional cost to you—when you click some of the ebook format links and purchase. Please know that commissions do not affect our opinions or evaluations. Readers must conduct their own research and exercise due diligence before making any purchases. Your decision to purchase something is entirely up to you, and you alone.

Disclaimer

THE CONTENT OF THIS BOOK IS FOR INFORMATIONAL PURPOSES ONLY. IT IS NOT INTENDED TO OFFER FINANCIAL OR CAREER ADVICE. The career and side hustle job ideas presented herein may be speculative, and none of the ideas shall be construed as guaranteed pathways to financial success. Readers must conduct their own rigorous research before making any job-related decisions.

CONTENTS

PART II
SIDE HUSTLES

PUBLISHER'S WEBSITE

For more information on artificial intelligence and machine learning, please visit us at **Nice Machine AI**.

INTRODUCTION

Greetings, Human!

The year is 2023—and the AI Automation Revolution is well underway!

If you're excited to explore the rapidly changing landscape of professional opportunities, then you've picked up the right book. Whether you're a young professional just starting out in the workforce or an employee considering a career pivot, *101: AI Job Ideas—from Careers to Side Hustles* offers an introductory primer that will help you kickstart your job-hunting journey.

The appeal of artificial intelligence and machine learning-related jobs is undeniable. And with this technology advancing so rapidly, there's tremendous demand for skilled professionals heading *into the future*—everything from healthcare, finance, entertainment, and so much more.

It's important to note that AI is not an industry but a transformative tool like the internet, significantly impacting almost every aspect of our lives. While traditional professional roles will undoubtedly disappear or change with this disruptive technology, it will also usher in new and exciting ways to earn income. These new opportunities will cater to various skill sets and interests, ranging from the technical know-how of data scientists to the communication and leadership skills of public speakers.

We believe the new AI job market will highly favor careers that require a combination of hard and soft skills. Hard skills require a strong command of technical fields such as mathematics, statistics, or programming, which involve expertise in coding languages like Python or R and libraries like TensorFlow or PyTorch. On the other hand, soft skills—also known as "the human touch"—require creativity, communication, and emotional intelligence, where the ability to solve problems and engage in effective interpersonal interactions with others takes priority. *(Sorry, Hal!)* Current examples of careers using both sets of skills include data storytellers, UX/UI designers, and AI ethicists.

In addition to a changing career landscape, gig and freelance jobs —aka "side hustles"—will also unlock new income-generating possibilities. For example, creatives and go-getters can employ generative AI to speed up client ideation, writing, and design efforts—while others may opt to develop and manage chatbots.

So, whether you're seeking a traditional 9-to-5 career or a side hustle that works better with your schedule, *opportunities abound!* Please note, however, that it's imperative to continually upskill your knowledge base *(especially with the rise of the machines!)* to stay competitive and employable. Fortunately, in 2023, companies are increasingly investing in AI training programs to help meet the workplace demands ahead. If your company does not offer such training—or you are currently unemployed—we suggest exploring online education through Coursera or Maven.

Without a doubt, AI is an exciting new tool for humankind. And with hard work, focus, and the human spark, we will continue to be the *masters* of our destiny.

Happy exploring!

I want to express my gratitude to my mother, who has been my biggest supporter in my writing journey, and to Alexis, my amazing girlfriend, who encouraged me to write the book. I am most grateful for both of your love and support.

PART I
CAREERS

AI CHATBOT DEVELOPER

Build chatbots with platforms like CustomGPT, Poe, Dialogflow, or Rasa and programming languages like Python and JavaScript. Market your chatbot development skills to retail, transportation, healthcare, finance, and other industries looking to optimize customer service and employee workflows.

AI CREATIVE DIRECTOR

Provide creative leadership to retail, sports, advertising, media & entertainment, and other industries. With generative AI (GenAI) and data-driven intel, craft targeted brand campaigns that help connect with customers.

AI DATA COMPLIANCE AUDITOR

Collaborate with data scientists and legal teams to audit artificial intelligence (AI) systems for accuracy, transparency, and fairness. Ensure ethical practices with machine learning (ML) models, utilizing an open-source software toolkit such as IBM AI Fairness 360. Offer your services to healthcare, legal, automotive, finance sectors, and more.

AI ETHICIST

Develop ethical guidelines and policies, educate and train management and employees, and engage with the public about the ethics of artificial intelligence. Ensure systems are used responsibly and aligned with an organization's core values. Apply your skills to technology, government, agriculture, finance, media industries, and more.

AI EVENT-OPS ORGANIZER

Elevate your event operations with AI tools such as ClickUp, Cvent, and Veritone, which can assist logistics and enhance the attendee experience through smart sensors and data analytics. Ensure a seamless event by managing vendors, location arrangements, guest lists, and staffing. Offer your services to companies hosting conferences, fundraisers, and corporate events.

AI FACILITIES MANAGER

Enhance facilities' energy consumption by harnessing the power of an AI and Internet of Things (IoT) platform like BrainCube to scrutinize sensor data. Analyze usage patterns to fine-tune heating, ventilation & air conditioning (HVAC), lighting, and other systems to curtail wastage. Extend your service of facility optimization to commercial real estate, manufacturing, technology sectors, and more.

AI FAN-OPS MANAGER

Revolutionize retail, sports, in-venue experiences, and more by leveraging an AI tool like Raydiant to execute real-time interactive customer experiences. Craft promotions and concessions to deliver personalized experiences that exceed customer expectations.

AI FARMING

Develop sustainable farming, harvesting, and planning methods with artificial intelligence. Apply deep learning to data gathered by mini "insect" robots to streamline farming processes and reduce costs so that local farmers can make informed, real-time decisions for the best way to manage their land.

AI HEALTHCARE DIAGNOSTICIAN

Enhance medical diagnostics with the help of AI, which can improve accuracy, efficiency, and accessibility. Platforms such as Qure.ai and Optellum can be utilized to develop clinical decision support systems that assist in interpreting complex scans and tests. Offer your expertise to healthcare companies that aim to enhance patient outcomes through both technology and the human touch.

AI HOSPITAL ADMINISTRATOR

Utilize AI techniques, such as predictive analytics, to manage hospital operations and resources, resulting in optimized patient outcomes. Strategize for the long term while handling daily needs, including staffing, inventory, and patient flow. Offer your management services to healthcare networks seeking to increase efficiency.

AI INVESTMENT ANALYST

For the world's markets (New York, London, Shanghai, Tokyo), use financial data insights, predictive algorithms, and backtesting to help guide and inform investment decisions. Create automated trading systems (bots) and help hedge funds, brokerages, and investment firms capitalize on AI.

AI LEGAL ASSISTANT

Optimize legal research, document preparation, and contract management with the help of AI-powered tools such as Kira, Writesonic, and LongShot. Speed up case preparation by fact-checking sources, researching relevant case law precedents, and drafting template documents, ultimately reducing the workload of attorneys. Offer your services to small and large-sized law firms seeking to simplify their legal workflows.

AI MACHINE MANAGER

For finance, healthcare, technology, retail, manufacturing, and other sectors, monitor and troubleshoot issues that may arise across various AI /ML applications in real-time. Use a tool like Hopsworks to monitor models and handle anomalies. Diagnose production models to ensure optimal performance.

AI MARKETING MANAGER

Oversee the development and implementation of AI-powered marketing strategies. Work closely with data scientists, engineers, and other marketing professionals to identify and leverage AI-driven insights to improve customer engagement, personalization, and campaign performance. Offer your services to companies that prioritize technology.

AI MEDIA COMMENTATOR

Communicate complex AI concepts in a digestible way to general audiences. Build a personal brand as a thought leader, demystifying artificial intelligence and its societal impacts. Partner with mainstream media, local news outlets, and social media influencer platforms seeking an expert to explain breaking news and trends.

AI POLICY EXPERT

Guide AI / ML innovation while mitigating the risks associated with these new technologies. Collaborate with organizations like the AI Policy Observatory to promote responsible practices to protect the public interest. Conduct research, propose regulations, and provide advisory services to policymakers and industry leaders from the government to technology-related companies.

AI-POWERED REALTOR

For residential and commercial real estate, assist buyers and sellers with transactions using tools like Zillow and Trulia. Generate property listings, schedule appointments, and provide market analysis. Use GenAI tools like Pixlr and Fotor to create beautiful photos for marketing.

AI PRODUCT DESIGNER

Create 3D modeling with design software such as Autodesk Fusion, Matterport, and Figma. Leverage robotics, valuable user feedback, and data-driven insights to speed up the product development cycle and create multiple iterations of product designs. Offer your services to travel, hospitality, manufacturing, retail, government sectors, and more.

AI PRODUCT RESEARCHER

Leverage data collection and management, machine learning frameworks, NLP, visualization, knowledge management, model deployment, and AI explainability tools to accelerate product development, enhance product features, and improve user experiences for automotive, finance, retail, manufacturing, healthcare sectors, and more.

AI RESEARCH ANALYST

Utilize large language models (LLMs — i.e. Claude, Bard, ChatGPT) and other AI tools to analyze data and develop innovative, tailored solutions to advance the understanding of artificial intelligence and its applications for businesses. Offer your services to healthcare, finance, retail, manufacturing, technology sectors, and more.

AI SALES ANALYTICS MANAGER

To help drive productivity and revenue growth for companies, use software platforms like Gong's Revenue Intelligence and Salesforce to analyze data, discover market trends, and uncover valuable consumer intelligence.

AI SOFTWARE DEVELOPER

Develop frameworks and infrastructure to facilitate artificial intelligence, machine learning, deep learning, and neural network systems with programming languages like Python and Java and development platforms like PyCaret. Create reusable libraries and pipelines to support in-house data science and ML teams. Provide services to technology, finance, automotive, manufacturing, media industries, and more.

AI SUPPLY CHAIN ANALYST

Utilize AI predictive analytic platforms like Coupa to improve inventory, logistics, and network flows. Apply simulation and generative planning techniques to identify cost savings and reduce risk in operations. Offer your skills to retail, manufacturing, distribution companies, and more.

AIR TRAFFIC CONTROLLER

Leverage AI systems to streamline operations at airports of all sizes. Enhance routing efficiency, boost capacity, and prevent flight conflicts. Employ smart systems that continuously adapt to real-time data, such as weather patterns and traffic flows, ensuring safe and efficient utilization of both airspace and tarmacs.

AR DESIGNER

Create immersive augmented reality (AR) experiences with tools like Unity and Apple ARKit for entertainment, education, retail, architecture, tourism sectors, and more. Develop branded games, facility tours, and interactive content that leave a lasting impression. Integrate Microsoft's Copilot AI platform into your workflows for a new collaborative office experience.

ASTRONAUT

Working with AI systems (*ahem—Hal 9000*), venture into space to conduct scientific research, gather data, and expand humanity's understanding of the universe.

AUTOMATION SPECIALIST

For finance, healthcare, transportation, manufacturing, and other sectors, streamline operations and achieve greater efficiencies with Robotic Process Automation (RPA) tools like UiPath, Automation Anywhere, and other workflow platforms. Improve productivity, reduce costs, and enhance customer experiences by designing bots and predictive processes that address repetitive workflows.

BIG DATA ENGINEER

Design and develop systems that handle large data pipelines while maintaining speed and stability across technology, finance, media, retail industries, and more. Conduct data analysis with statistical and AI models like Scikit-Learn and Apache Spark.

BUSINESS INTELLIGENCE ANALYST

Use a platform like Microsoft Power BI to collect, organize, and analyze business insight data to help organizations make better strategic decisions. Use data modeling, data mining, and other analytical techniques to identify trends and patterns in data sets to derive meaningful conclusions about business performance and opportunities. Offer your services to technology, retail, hospitality industries, and more.

CLOUD ENGINEER

Leverage automation, analytics, and security best practices on platforms like Amazon Web Services (AWS), Google Cloud, and Microsoft Azure. Architect low-latency, secure cloud environments with orchestration tools and infrastructure-as-code techniques. Help technology, finance, retail, media sectors, and more migrate their workloads and processes to the cloud.

COMPUTER SCIENTIST

Leverage machine learning and neural networks alongside robust programming languages like Python, R, and Java to devise solutions for complex issues companies are facing. Offer your skills to technology, IT, finance, manufacturing, government, transportation industries, and more.

COMPUTER VISION ENGINEER

Use an AI-powered solution like OpenCV to analyze images and videos for recognition, classification, and quality assurance tasks. Develop computer vision capabilities like object detection and localization that can be applied to various domains, from technology to transportation to the government.

CYBERSECURITY ANALYST

Ensure the safety of networks, devices, individuals, and information by utilizing Security Information and Event Management (SIEM) tools such as Darktrace and Sentinel to prevent unauthorized access and cyberattacks. Offer real-time anomaly detection and response abilities to technology companies like Google, IBM, Microsoft, Apple, and Meta.

DATA STORYTELLER

Transform raw data into compelling narratives and visualizations, conveying insights to stakeholders with tools like Tableau, Looker, Datawrapper, and Smartdraw. Contextualize analyses into digestible dashboards, reports, and presentations that drive informed decision-making and strategy. Offer your visual storytelling skills to businesses that want to communicate complex ideas as simply as possible.

DEV-OPS ENGINEER

Improve software delivery and infrastructure changes by incorporating process automation and monitoring tools such as Moogsoft AIOps and Dynatrace. Enhance Continuous Integration and Continuous Delivery/Deployment (CI/CD) pipelines by integrating predictive intelligence to detect and resolve operational issues promptly. Provide your expertise to engineering teams across sectors seeking to enhance release cycles securely.

IOT DEVELOPER

Harness the power of edge computing to create intelligent Internet of Things (IoT) devices and systems for retail, agriculture, healthcare, manufacturing, government sectors, and more. Leverage a framework like TensorFlow Lite to develop, design, and test embedded systems to provide real-time responsiveness.

LEGAL AI SPECIALIST

Utilize programming languages such as Python and JavaScript to handle complex legal and intellectual property matters that require tailored solutions. Create natural language processing (NLP) and machine learning systems for intellectual property (IP) litigation, contract review, and e-discovery.

MECHANICAL ENGINEER

For transportation, manufacturing sectors, and more, leverage AI to optimize the entire process of designing, simulating, manufacturing, and testing mechanical systems by utilizing a tool like Ansys Simulation. Boost the overall efficiency, accuracy, and performance of various applications, including robotics, vehicles, medical devices, and smart products.

MACHINE LEARNING ENGINEER

Develop AI models with Python's Scikit-Learn and TensorFlow. Automate analysis with Apache Spark and interpret results through data visualization to gain valuable insights. Keep a close eye on model drift to ensure smooth operation of machine learning pipelines. Offer your skills to technology, manufacturing, finance, healthcare sectors, and more.

MEDIATOR

For legal, technology, automotive, manufacturing, government sectors, and more, apply communication and leadership skills to facilitate discussion between conflicting parties to reach mutual agreements and resolutions. Conduct research and implement solutions with various GenAI tools (i.e. Bard, Writesonic, etc.)

NLP TRAINER

Use a Python library like Gensim to harness language models to elevate human-machine interaction. Annotate conversational data to refine natural speech comprehension and cultivate robust natural language AI systems. Offer your skills to technology, R & D, customer service, finance sectors, and more.

OCEAN CLEANUP TECHNICIAN

Help clean our precious oceans by operating AI-powered waste removal systems like RanMarine's WasteShark. Maintain pollution-reducing drones, offering expertise to environmental organizations and corporations committed to helping the environment.

ROBOTICS ENGINEER

Design, develop, and evaluate robotic systems enriched with artificial intelligence and automation. Produce adaptable and intelligent robots with tools like ROS and MATLAB to incorporate functions like computer vision, navigation, manipulation, and environmental awareness. Provide customized robotics solutions for various industries, including manufacturing, medicine, transportation, consumer applications, and more.

SMART CITY PLANNER

Model future urban center designs using AI simulation and generative techniques for livability and sustainability with platforms like Agora and Hasso Plattner Institute. Guide long-term city and rural planning by balancing economic development with environmental stewardship.

SOCIAL MEDIA MANAGER

Employ tools like Hootsuite, Sprout Social, Writesonic, ChatGPT, and others to generate engaging social media content, schedule posts at optimal times, monitor conversations, analyze data, and target ads effectively. Offer your skills to retail, e-commerce, technology, finance, healthcare, entertainment, hospitality, automotive industries, and more.

SOFTWARE BUSINESS DEVELOPER

Bridge the gap between AI software development and a company's goals and objectives. Use business acumen and communication skills to develop and implement sales strategies and manage relationships with key stakeholders—from software teams to management to customers. Offer your services to technology-related companies.

STATISTICIAN

For agriculture, transportation, finance sectors, and more, apply statistical and machine learning algorithms, such as random forests and neural networks, to uncover business intelligence. Identify connections between departments and other variables to create easy-to-understand reports that help facilitate strategic decision-making.

UX/UI DESIGNER

Create intuitive, user-friendly interfaces for AI-related products leveraging data and A/B testing with a tool like Adobe XD. Focus on customer needs through iterative design, prototyping, and user research. Provide your technical prowess and human touch to technology, media, finance, healthcare, retail companies, and more.

VOICE INTERFACE DESIGNER

For consumer electronics, banking & finance, automotive industries, and more, leverage a tool like Rhasspy to craft engaging conversational dialogues, intuitive system prompts, and memorable voice personalities for various applications. Refine your creations through iterative prototyping and user testing, ensuring a natural and intuitive experience for human-machine interactions.

VR DESIGNER

For education, gaming & entertainment, architecture, engineering & construction industries, etc., create breathtaking worlds with a virtual reality (VR) tool like Unity. Design and oversee natural interactions, physics, locomotion, and autonomy through simulations and machine learning that create highly immersive experiences.

PART II

SIDE HUSTLES

AD CAMPAIGN MANAGER

Craft advertising material for local small businesses with GenAI tools like Canva and Kittl for art & design and Writesonic, LongShot, and Jasper for content marketing and copywriting. Utilize AdCreative.AI to tailor and optimize campaigns. Provide your services to restaurants, auto shops, barbers, and more.

AFFILIATE MARKETER

Market products or services of other businesses and earn commissions for each sale you generate online. Use AI tools to create video and blogging content, keyword targeting, link building, and website optimization.

AI CONSULTANT

Assist companies in implementing solutions that boost productivity through platforms such as DataRobot and H2O.ai. Conduct feasibility studies and offer strategic recommendations. Depending on your expertise, market your consulting services to startups, retail, travel sectors, and more via local business networking groups and meetups.

AI CONTENT DETECTIVE

Use tools like DuckDuckGoose to identify synthetic content, commonly known as "deepfakes," or Red Points to help safeguard copyrights online. Help authors, book publishers, musicians, attorneys, media companies, and other content creators scan the internet to protect and preserve their intellectual property (IP).

AI CONTENT SUPERVISOR

Ensure AI-generated content with proofreading and fact-checking services. Utilize tools such as CustomGPT, Writesonic, Grammarly, and more to add a human review process to ensure brand consistency, readability, and factual accuracy for clients. Offer your skills to education, marketing & advertising, media & publishing, legal sectors, and more.

AI DATA PRIVACY CONSULTANT

With tools like IBM Watson, Microsoft Azure AI, and Google Cloud AI, conduct privacy audits and risk assessments to help organizations ethically manage consumer data and comply with regulations. Help large and small-sized companies build trust with their customers and the public through transparency.

AI EXPLAINER PRODUCER

With or without your face, use an AI tool like Loom to produce videos that simplify concepts and repetitive tasks for audiences. Promote your production services to startups, travel, real estate companies, and others.

AI INTERIOR DESIGNER

Offer customized interior design services for homes and businesses with an AI-powered tool like Homestyler. Design spaces that match your client's unique style and requirements. Promote your services to residential and commercial property owners, builders, and realtors.

AI LEGACY CONTENT MANAGER

Organize videos, photos, important documents, letters, and more with AI-powered platforms like PhotoPrism and MyHeritage Photo Enhancer. Digitize aging media and preserve important memories for clients looking to archive their collections securely. Promote your content management service through Instagram, Fiverr, Upwork, and other platforms.

AI PHOTOGRAPHER

Edit and enhance photos with robust platforms like Runway and Adobe Firefly. Provide photography services for e-commerce, retail, automotive, realtors, stock footage libraries, and more. Use AI to tag, sort, and enhance large volumes of images for your clients efficiently.

AI-POWERED CODE REVIEWER

Review and improve code quality with human oversight and AI tools like DeepCode and Codacy. Offer your services to a wide variety of industries requiring software development.

AI-POWERED CUSTOMER SERVICE REP

Work from home and offer customer service support for companies that use live-agent AI chatbot platforms such as LiveChat or Tidio. For retail, e-commerce, and other industries provide invaluable human assistance when the bots do not have the answers. (*We will not be replaced!*)

AI-POWERED PRODUCT REVIEWER

Write product reviews and recommendations using AI tools like Writesonic and Claude. Offer your services to e-commerce stores, review websites, focus groups, marketing agencies, and more.

AI PROMPT ENGINEER

Craft tailored AI content prompts optimizing system output for different applications and industries with a blend of creative writing and technical mastery with LLMs like Bard, Claude, or ChatGPT. Market your prompt engineering services to prompt libraries and companies deploying customer service chatbots, personal voice assistants, and other use cases in marketing & advertising, education, finance, human resources, healthcare, and more.

AI SEO SPECIALIST

Help e-commerce, travel companies, and more improve their search engine rankings and increase traffic by optimizing their websites with tools like KWFinder, Semrush, and Ahrefs. Offer ongoing research, optimization, backlink strategies, and popular hashtag usage to companies that need assistance boosting their market awareness and customer conversion rates.

AI TESTER

Sign up for in-person and online participation studies related to natural language processing, machine learning, and other AI systems. Evaluate new products for companies like Google, Microsoft, Amazon, Meta, and IBM. Explore opportunities directly through companies' websites, LinkedIn, Indeed, and elsewhere.

AI TRANSLATOR

Use tools like Veed, DeepL, or Google Translate to offer translation services to small and large-sized companies that operate in multiple languages.

AI TRAVEL AGENT

Use Google, Expedia, and Wanderbot to customize travel itineraries (flights, hotels, rentals, activities, etc.). Cater to leisure, corporate, or luxury markets that expect high-end personalization and top-notch service. Work with existing travel agencies, both locally and globally.

AI TUTOR

Develop customized learning experiences for students with a tutoring tool like Knewton. Create interactive lesson plans, track student progress, and provide feedback. Offer courses through Zoom and YouTube and explore partnership opportunities with online schools like Coursera, Udemy, Maven, and others.

AI WARDROBE STYLIST

Provide personalized fashion recommendations with a style analysis tool like Wardrobe AI. Suggest new styles, outfits, and shopping ideas based on your client's preferences. Promote your tailored styling services through virtual consultations on Instagram, YouTube, and more.

ALGORITHM DEVELOPER

Design and implement powerful algorithms to address complex challenges for clients. Leverage proficiency in programming languages like Python, Java, and C++ to create efficient machine-learning models and data processing pipelines tailored to specific client needs. Market your skills to technology companies, startups, or freelance gig platforms like Fiverr.

BLOCKCHAIN DEVELOPER

Paired with AI, utilize cryptography, consensus protocols, and smart contracts via programming languages like Solidity and C++ to create and execute blockchain applications. Offer expertise to finance, manufacturing, security, transportation, and other sectors that want to leverage cutting-edge technology for supply chain control, credentialing, and more.

BOOK AUTHOR

Use AI tools such as Writesonic, Claude, and ChatGPT to help develop and flesh out drafts. Create print and ebooks with software such as Vellum and Canva. Self-publish through a platform like Amazon Kindle Direct Publishing (KDP). Additionally, collaborate with other authors and help them launch books that cater to specific niches, such as large print books for seniors, daily journals, educational workbooks, or culinary books.

BOOKKEEPER

Streamline financial modeling, data analysis, and workflows. Utilize NLP, ML, and data visualization to develop custom formulas, macros, and add-ins with Excel or Google Sheets. Market your skills to small businesses to help them stay on top of their cash flow and improve productivity.

BRAND CONSULTANT

Craft names and brand identities for businesses with tools such as Namelix and Adobe Firefly. Conduct market research and analysis to help position and differentiate brands in their respective market segments. Offer packages to startups, technology, media, retail companies, and others seeking a unique look and feel.

BUSINESS PLAN CONSULTANT

Improve client business plans and proposals with writing tools like Grammarly and Copy.ai and fact-check citations with LongShot. Provide your services to entrepreneurs who want to multiply their time, enabling them to concentrate on investor pitches, marketing & sales efforts.

CAREER COACH

Utilize AI tools such as Bard, Claude, and TopResume to help optimize resumes. Use LinkedIn, Medium, YouTube, and other platforms to market to young professionals and career switchers as potential clients.

CAREGIVER

Provide baby boomers with physical activity, conversation, AI/tech assistance, and compassion that machines cannot replicate. Depending on your client's preferences and abilities, offer companionship during walks at the local park or over coffee at the nearest Starbucks. Market your services to busy professionals and families looking for alternative care options for their aging loved ones.

CHILDREN'S BOOK DESIGNER

Create designs for children's book authors with AI software tools such as Adobe Firefly, Canva, and Stable Diffusion. Offer coloring and activity books for sale through Amazon KDP. Market your services on YouTube, Instagram, LinkedIn, Fiverr, and elsewhere.

COPYWRITER

Write tailored blogs, product descriptions, and email marketing campaigns for clients using tools like Writesonic and LongShot. Provide copywriting services to entrepreneurs, restaurants, advertising agencies, media companies, and more.

DATA ANNOTATOR

Use Python, R, SQL, and Excel to gather, examine, and clarify data. Employ statistical analysis, data visualization, data mining, and predictive modeling to draw insights from intricate datasets that benefit clients. Offer your skills to retail, healthcare, agriculture, automotive, finance industries, and more.

FACELESS YOUTUBER

Use AI tools like Fliki, Pictory, and Synthesia to produce "faceless" video and audio content. Share your expertise on topics without showing your face through text captions, narration, and stock footage on YouTube and Instagram. In addition to helping protect your privacy, this approach focuses on the subject matter rather than the personality behind it. Market your video production skills to retail, realtors, restaurants, car dealerships, and more.

GENERATIVE ARTIST

Generate custom 2D and 3D digital art assets for film/TV, gaming, virtual reality (VR), and augmented reality (AR) with tools like Runway's Stable Diffusion and Motion Brush, Krea, and Midjourney. Offer your AI-generated art skills on a freelance platform like Fiverr or NFT marketplaces like OpenSea. Through a site like LinkedIn, network with advertising execs, filmmakers, game developers, technologists, and local entrepreneurs who need high-quality, royalty-free content.

GENERATIVE COMIC CREATOR

Create comics, cartoons, graphic memoirs, and branded entertainment with illustration tools such as Adobe Firefly, DALLE-3, and ComicsMaker.AI to bring your ideas to life. Utilize an LLM like Claude to assist with outlining and drafting. Promote your new service through social media and monetize it through subscription-revenue platforms like Webtoons and Tapas.

GHOSTWRITER

Use AI writing tools such as Writesonic, Rytr, Grammarly, and others to craft blog articles and books for clients. Focus on public figures, influencers, business leaders, content marketers, and others who want to offer high-quality content to their target audience.

GRAPHIC DESIGNER

Create customized logos, graphics, posters, and other visual assets for clients using design platforms like Canva, Kittl, and Adobe Firefly. Market your design skills to retailers, travel companies, e-commerce, and many more.

HEALTH COACH

Offer personalized health and nutrition guidance with a tool like FitnessAI to analyze client data from apps and wearables. Tailor supplement recommendations, diet plans, and workout routines to each person's history, biomarkers, and objectives. Promote your services to health-conscious individuals who desire both a high-touch and high-tech approach.

MEDIA PRODUCER

Use a robust editing tool like Clipchamp to enhance YouTube and Instagram videos, promos, event slideshows, and more. Or use a tool like Steve AI to create videos from blog posts. Offer your services to social media influencers, small businesses, wedding planners, travel companies, and more.

MOTION GRAPHICS DESIGNER

Create stunning motion graphics and special effects with Adobe After Effects and Stability for Blender. Contact event planners, video production firms, digital agencies, social media influencers, and more to offer your expertise in creating dynamic content that engages audiences.

MUSIC PRODUCER

Generate custom beats and samples for clients with tools like Veed, Magenta Studio, Google DeepMind, and AIVA. Promote your AI-infused melodies, rhythms, and jams to wedding planners, event management companies, and more. License your tracks through Artlist and Epidemic Sound.

NO-CODE / LOW-CODE PROGRAMMER

Create processes, apps, and knowledge bases for clients without knowing how to code (*although it's helpful to have a basic understanding!*) with platforms such as Bubble, Make, CustomGPT, and Zapier. Offer no-code/low-code development services to startups and others wanting to automate workflows.

PODCAST SUMMARIZER

Utilize a tool like Melville AI to create informative show notes, episode summaries, and bullet points for podcast audiences. Focus on podcasters who want a third party to help ensure quality control.

PODCASTER

Create and produce a podcast series using Descript, Adobe Podcast, and Buzzsprout tools. Discuss topics you're passionate about, such as entrepreneurship, career, health & wellness, relationships, film/TV, and more, on platforms like Apple Podcasts for Creators. Add Patreon if you'd like to consider listener contribution options.

PUBLIC SPEAKING COACH

Help professionals improve their leadership and communication skills. Attend weekly speaking group meetings with your clients—like The Speakers Alliance or Toastmasters. Use an AI-powered tool such as Orai to help them practice between sessions. Promote your coaching services on LinkedIn, Twitter, YouTube, and Facebook.

SHOP CREATOR

With the help of AI tools like Canva and Adobe Firefly, create customized product designs on an e-commerce platform like Etsy. Upload your creations for print-on-demand products (i.e., t-shirts, mugs, stationery, phone cases, pillows, etc.) Etsy will handle the entire fulfillment process, from customer orders to shipping.

TRANSCRIPTIONIST

Convert audio recordings, including podcasts, interviews, speeches, and virtual meetings, into text with transcription tools like Otter.ai and Fireflies. Produce precise and time-stamped transcripts like executive summaries or blog posts. Promote your transcription services to legal, medical, media & entertainment, education sectors, and more.

UAV OPERATOR

Operate unmanned aerial vehicles (UAVs) to collect data and conduct surveillance. Utilize onboard AI systems to aid in navigation, object detection, and collision avoidance. Ensure safe, legal operation while meeting data collection objectives. Offer your services to agriculture, public safety, delivery & logistics, environmental sectors, and more.

VIRTUAL ASSISTANT

Provide administrative, technical, and creative assistance to clients remotely. Use platforms like Zirtual and Fancy Hands to offer email management, scheduling, social media management, GenAI content creation services, and more.

VIRTUAL EVENT HOST

Organize and execute virtual events with platforms like vFairs and InEvent. Engage virtual or in-person hybrid audiences with interactive features like live polls, chat, and Q&A sessions. Assume the role of a master of ceremonies for conferences, trade shows, job fairs, team-building events, and other group-oriented occasions.

VOICEOVER TALENT

Use AI voice studio platforms such as Descript, Murf, and Speechify to provide voiceovers, podcast/audiobook recordings, and more. Offer your voiceover services to small and large media companies, authors, bloggers, political campaigns, and more on a contract basis.

WEB DESIGNER

Develop niche sites for clients seeking to establish an online presence and generate income with AI site builders like Squarespace or Durable. Offer your web development services to small businesses, e-commerce, retail, and many more.

WEB MONITOR

Keep track of brands, keywords, trends, and online sentiment with AI analytics and alert services such as Browse.ai and Mention. Market your services to marketing agencies, realtors, law firms, media outlets, political organizations, and more so they can make well-informed decisions based on real-time insights.

THAT'S A WRAP!

Thanks for flipping through *101 AI Jobs—From Careers to Side Hustles*! We wish you the best as you continue exploring new and exciting ways to make a living in our increasingly machine-driven world.

ABOUT THE PUBLISHER

Nice Machine AI Publishing provides news, tools, and tips to professionals who want to learn more about our changing, automation-driven workplace.

Sign up for our newsletter here:

https://nicemachineai.bio.link

Or check us out on:

linkedin.com/in/nice-machine-ai